FORGIVEN

Tikesha McNulty

KP PUBLISHING COMPANY

Centenary Translation: THE NEW TESTAMENT IN MODERN ENGLISH by Helen Barrett Montgomery, 1924. Scriptures marked MKJV are taken from the MODERN KING JAMES VERSION (MKJV): Scripture taken from the Holy Bible, MODERN KING JAMES VERSION copyright© 1962—1998 by Jay P. Green, Sr. Used by permission of the copyright holder.

Scriptures marked AMP are taken from the AMPLIFIED BIBLE (AMP): Scripture taken from the AMPLIFIED® BIBLE, Copyright © 1954, 1958, 1962, 1964, 1965, 1987 by the Lockman Foundation Used by Permission. www.Lockman.org

Scripture quotations marked (TLB) are taken from The Living Bible copyright © 1971. Used by permission of Tyndale House Publishers, Carol Stream, Illinois 60188. All rights reserved.

ISBN: 979-8-9869907-6-7 (Paperback)
ISBN: 979-8-9869907-7-4 (eBook)
Library of Congress Control Number: Pending

Editor: KP Publishing Services
Cover Design: Meilani Darby
Interior Design: Jennifer Houle
Literary Director: Sandra James

Published by:

KP Publishing Company
Publisher of Fiction, Nonfiction & Children's Books
Valencia, CA 91355
www.kp-pub.com

Printed in the United States of America

CONTENTS

FROM THE AUTHOR
TIKESHA MCNULTY

To achieve your highest potential and become your best self, you must be honest with where you are. You must also be willing to release what's holding you back and forgive any offense that has taken you, hostage. Maya Angelou suggested that forgiveness is, "One of the greatest gifts you can give yourself." Gandhi believed that "it is the attribute of the strong." Oscar Wilde even said, "Always forgive your enemies. Nothing will annoy them so much."

I understand forgiveness isn't always easy; it's a process. There are going to be days when you feel you are free from the offense and then there will be days where you may wrestle with the pain. It's all ok, it's part of the process. But I want you to understand that forgiveness is the key to unlocking doors in your life that were never meant to be closed. It is essential, an act of love and strength. It's a gift that we as an individual benefit from.

I speak from experience. Let me tell you, my life hasn't been a walk in the park. Everything life could have thrown at me came at me with full force. From betrayal, cheating, domestic violence, failed marriages, and depression, that's just to name a few! Through my adversity, I had to study, meditate, and implement the act of forgiveness. Everything I talk about in this book, I've had to walk it out myself. This journey has not been simple, but it was necessary for my growth. It was through the love and understanding of God that I am where I am today. I had to learn His perspective of forgiveness. My hope is that this book does the same for you. You are never alone. We are on this journey of becoming—together.

I know your mind instantly started thinking of millions of reasons why you shouldn't have to forgive. I get it! I do! I understand. But you also have a choice. Everything in life is about choices and opportunities. It is a defining moment for you. Don't miss it. Seize it. Forgiveness isn't about anyone else but you.

As you continue to read through this book, it is my prayer that you are able to let the pain and the perpetrator(s) go and that you walk gloriously into your freedom from the bondage of the past. Thank you for taking the first step into becoming the best version of yourself.

LET'S ERADICATE UNFORGIVENESS

I know you feel that you are justified in harboring unforgiveness, and as you continue reading, you will realize that holding on keeps you bound. You will get to a place where, it no longer hurts; or that you are no longer numb. We are going to get there, I promise. However, in order not to waste time and for you to experience real results and breakthroughs, we must start with YOU and ME.

> *Disclaimer: If you don't believe that all things are possible with God, then put the book down right here. Unfortunately, it will not change you or benefit you in any way because you aren't ready to dig deep. You MUST be ready to go back and pull up every root of unforgiveness planted in the secret garden of your mind and in your life. They MUST go.*

On this journey of letting go, we will discover a powerful truth. We have to take personal inventory and be accountable for ourselves.

1

Doing this will require you to be honest with yourself. Are you ready to do that? The beauty is you don't have to pretend or impress anyone. It's just you and God, and He already knows. He is going to walk with you and love you through this process, so be patient.

As you know, there are thousands of books written on the subject of forgiveness. I'm sure you're probably wondering how this one is different. Well, in this book, we will break down various aspects of forgiveness and how to tackle each one. Not only that, I'm going to hold your hand and walk you through it. We will go through this journey together and celebrate your freedom and victory at the end.

If you want to live the life you are destined to live, you must first believe that you can forgive. That may seem odd, and sometimes the pain is so deep that we can't see past the fog. We wonder how we can ever let it go, but you can—and you can be free. You just have to know it's possible and desire the possibility. God will only give you what you can wholeheartedly believe. You must believe that you can forgive that person who molested you; or your little sister for stealing your clothes or for stealing your man. You can forgive that person who killed your loved one or even that person who committed adultery on you with a family member. Guess what? YOU WILL GET THERE! But if you choose to say, "Girl, you don't know what they did, or the pain I've endured. The humiliation and the loss are just too much!" Then you're right, you won't be able to get over it. Rehearsing the pain will keep you on an emotional hamster wheel. Give yourself permission to be free.

Next, you must choose to forgive. Forgiveness is a choice that requires action on your part. You must be an active participant in this process. Otherwise, buy this book for a friend who believes this will work for them. Let's explain what that means. The Word is clear about forgiving your brother (Sisters, you all are not off the hook. The word "brother" is inclusive of everyone.)

> *"And in wrath his master turned him over to the torturers (jailers until he paid all that he owed. My heavenly Father will also do the same to [every one of] you, if each of you does not forgive his brother from your heart."*
> **Matthew 18:34-35 (AMP)**

One of the results of not forgiving others is that you will not be forgiven. If I'm not forgiven, then what? I say this all the time, "Ain't nobody worth going to hell over." Nothing said about us or done to us directly or indirectly is worth going to hell for. Yet, this is exactly what unforgiveness produces: NOTHING! NO FRUIT. NO GROWTH. NO FREEDOM. ABSOLUTELY NOTHING!

If you believe that God can do all things, if you are willing to release control, then keep reading. This book is anointed to knock down barriers, strongholds, and demonic influences. If you let it, it can help you break anything unhealthy that's preventing you from letting go and eradicating unforgiveness.

There are five sections in this book that will help guide you on your journey to forgiveness. If you feel the need to take more time in a particular section, do so. Think of this as your own personal journey toward forgiveness and healing.

While going through this forgiveness journey, I recommend keeping a journal or notebook. It will be good for you to write down your reflections, feelings, and downloads from God. There will be sections within the book where you can take a moment to pause, reflect, and write down your thoughts and feelings. This will also be a valuable resource for you to reflect on later to assess the progress that you've made along the way.

SECTION 1 –
I SURVIVED

I admit that I had feelings of anger, shame, and guilt from my past. I struggled with the idea for a long time and didn't want to forgive. I honestly believed that they did not deserve it.

> *He did not retaliate when he was insulted, nor*
> *threaten revenge when he suffered. He left his case*
> *in the hands of God, who always judges fairly. 24*
> *He personally carried our sins in his body on the*
> *cross so that we can be dead to sin and live for what*
> *is right. By his wounds you are healed.*
>
> **1 Peter 2:23-24 (NLT)**

Who are "They," you ask? "They" are all those that abused me as a child, mistreated me, misunderstood me, took me for granted, cheated on me, and got another woman pregnant while still married to me. The list could go on (but that's another book). How long is YOUR "They" list? Take some time to write down your "They," List. Who are "They" and what did "They" do to you? This may take you a few minutes or a few days. Take as much or as little time as you need. Please know it's ok if you get emotional through this process, but it is necessary.

I understand it is hard to forgive someone who has hurt you; revenge seems easier. Staying mad and bitter is comfortable, but that's not what Jesus wants us to do. As Christians, we know we are supposed to follow Jesus, but during stressful times, this can be hard to do. Following Jesus will take courage, perseverance, and trust.

You see, forgiveness is more than a choice . . . forgiveness is a calling. By forgiving, I was able to release my pain and trust God to vindicate me. By me releasing unforgiveness, it didn't excuse what they had done; but it allowed me to stop being the victim. It allowed me to take the focus off the hurt and offense, putting my focus back on Christ. What would Jesus do? That's a question I have to constantly ask myself daily. Remember, we are called to be an example of who He is and how He loves. God really does know our hearts, our motives, and our intentions. He only looks at the heart.

If you've been hurt and want to work towards forgiveness, I encourage you to do the following:

1. Pray about the offense and learn how the act of forgiveness can be empowering. Don't know how to pray? Just begin talking to God, or ask someone to pray with you.

2. Get a few scriptures on forgiveness. Below are
   some scriptures to help get you started.

*Our Father in heaven, may your name be kept
holy. May your Kingdom come soon. May your will
be done on earth, as it is in heaven. Give us today
the food we need, and forgive us our sins, as we
have forgiven those who sin against us. And don't
let us yield to temptation, but rescue us from the
evil one.*

Matthew 6:10-13

*Make allowance for each other's faults and forgive
anyone who offends you. Remember, the Lord
forgave you, so you must forgive others.*

Colossians 3:13

*But when you are praying, first forgive anyone you
are holding a grudge against, so that your Father in
heaven will forgive your sins, too."*

Mark 11:25

*For this is my blood, which confirms the covenant
between God and his people. It is poured out as a
sacrifice to forgive the sins of many.*

Matthew 26:28

3. Understand that it's normal for negative feelings to arise when we are hurt. But you must choose to let it go.

4. Talk to someone you trust about what you are experiencing.

5. DON'T RUSH! Forgiveness is a process. We have to walk in forgiveness daily. You must first choose to forgive yourself, then you can forgive others.

JOURNALING SESSION

Take a moment to write down in your journal the following:

• What do I need to forgive myself for?

_____

_____

_____

_____

• What do I need to forgive others for?

_____

_____

_____

_____

_____

Ask God to help you. Be honest with any unforgiveness you may have towards others and even yourself. You must believe that God is who He says He is. God does not lie. Allow yourself to receive the gift of forgiveness and to also give it to others in return. The source of EVERYTHING is God and God alone. Let the Lord perform a spiritual strip search that will only be between you and Him.

1. Honor the fact that you are becoming a better person as a result of making the choice to forgive.

FORGIVENESS PRODUCES FREEDOM

Forgiveness will open the door to freedom from past hurts.

Questions to ask yourself:
1. Does forgiveness come quickly for you, or is it something you have to work towards?
2. Have you ever been offered forgiveness by someone who has hurt you?
3. How did receiving forgiveness from someone else make you feel?
4. Why does forgiveness matter to you? To God? To others?

Write out the steps you will take to forgive.

_____

_____

_____

_____

_____

_____

Let people say whatever they want because, in the grand scheme of things, it really doesn't matter. If you genuinely have a relationship with God, you know that it is only what He thinks that matters. Release everyone who has ever wronged you. Those who've spoken against you, lied, slandered, misused, and taken you for granted. For everyone who broke your heart, even the ones who smiled in your face while they wronged you, release it. Stop and cast down every vain imagination that has tried to exalt itself against the Word of God!

> *Casting down imaginations and every high thing*
> *that exalteth itself against the knowledge of God,*
> *and bringing into captivity every thought to the*
> *obedience of Christ.*
> **2 Corinthians 10:5 CKJV**

You were created with purpose on purpose. You are destined for greatness. Your life, your time, and your purpose are not games to be played. Your impact is not a game. According to your faith, be it unto YOU! Do you want to live an abundant, fulfilled life? Or do you want to stay bound, stuck, and unfulfilled because you feel justified in unforgiveness? It is about being truly authentic and transparent with your Abba Father, the Lord Jesus, and the Holy Spirit.

Unforgiveness is something that is deeply rooted and can only be released by the power of the Holy Spirit. Often, we don't know the root of the unforgiveness or where it started. It has been embedded in us or may have come through our bloodline.

MOMENTS OF REFLECTION

Take the Time to Worship

- Spend some time in worship, thanksgiving, and blessing His Holy name.
- Take the time to thank God that you made it through this past week and that He is guiding you through your journey to forgiveness.
- You can make this a day of worship

If you can't think of any worship songs, here are some suggestions:

"You Are Welcome" Psalmist Raine

"Psalm 23 (I Am Not Alone" [Live at Linger Conference] People & Songs featuring Josh Sherman

"Change Me" Tamala Mann

"My Worship" Phil Thompson

"You Can Just Rest" Jenn Johnson and Hunter Thompson

"Jesus We Love You" Isabel Davis

MEDITATE ON GOD'S WORD

Spend some time meditating on God's word. It could be for an hour or even a day. Take the time to meditate on His word and reflect on the people you are forgiving. Rejoice in the Lord and again I say rejoice! Read:

> *As far as the east is from the west, so far has He removed our transgressions from us.*
>
> **Psalm 103:12 TLV**

> *For if you forgive men for their sins, your heavenly Father will also forgive you. But if you do not forgive men for their sins, neither will your Father forgive your sins.*
>
> **Matthew 6:14-15 MEV**

> *Take heed to yourselves. "If your brother sins against you, rebuke him. And if he repents, forgive him. If he sins against you seven times in a day, and seven times in a day turns to you, saying, 'I repent,' you must forgive him."*
>
> **Luke 17:3-4 MEV**

SECTION 2 – HOW DO I FORGIVE EVEN THOUGH I DON'T WANT TO?

So they sent word to Joseph, saying, "Your father commanded us before he died, saying, 'You are to say to Joseph, "I beg you, please forgive the transgression of your brothers and their sin, for they did you wrong."' Now, please forgive the transgression of the servants of the God of your father." And Joseph wept when they spoke to him. Then his brothers went and fell down before him [in confession]; then they said, "Behold, we are your servants (slaves)."

Genesis 50:16-18 AMP

15

Joseph's story is a notable example of a bloodline that was flowing with unforgiveness. His brothers harbored an offense against him, which resulted in Joseph being thrown in a pit. Joseph could have made the choice to operate in unforgiveness, but instead he chose to trust God. He released everyone who offended him. Imagine your brothers or any family member, trying to kill you and sell you off. Joseph could have (and rightfully so) become bitter or even lost his mind. When you allow that type of pain to fester in your heart you will never be free. It would be difficult to obtain your destiny or purpose.

Joseph did not allow unforgiveness to stop him from reaching his ultimate destiny. He saved a nation and his family. Imagine if he had not forgiven them. An entire nation and bloodline would have perished. My question is: how many people or nations are waiting on you? The Lord cannot trust you with mysteries and insights to help others if you can't forgive.

He can't trust you to be a distribution center and risk you holding back resources from someone you are offended by. It's not about you. It's about the Kingdom.

Release people and yourself. I promise, you will feel better after doing so. Besides, nine out of ten times, that person you're mad at or holding unforgiveness against isn't even thinking about you. For all you know they may have gone before the Lord, repented and moved on while you're still stuck.

We've all heard the saying, "You need to forgive and forget." When someone hurts you, do you want to forgive that person? Forgiving seems almost unnatural, right?

Here are six reasons why you should forgive someone, even when you don't want to do so.

1. It doesn't mean what they did was ok, nor does it mean they will be allowed back into your life. Forgiveness means you've made peace with the pain and you are ready to let it go and move on.

2. Forgiveness does not belong to the offender; this is what we must do for ourselves. Not forgiving is like giving someone free room and board in your heart and emotions. It is like being trapped in the jail cell, locked up in bitterness and serving time for someone else's crime. It is your choice to either dwell on the pain caused by others or free yourself for the sake of your destiny.

3. Know that the weak-minded will never forgive, they don't have the capacity to. Forgiveness is the attribute of an active, determined person who faces their pain head-on and takes the necessary steps to move on.

4. Forgiveness is not about the other person. Forgiveness is about you. Holding will never

make you feel better. Begin by forgiving
yourself and keep on moving.

5.   Forgiving another person is an act of love. Once
     forgiveness is achieved, you are sure to find that
     sense of peace that you longed for.

6.   Forgiveness is a choice. In making a decision,
     you are refusing to allow what happened to you
     to have rule over you. While it did happen and
     it may still hurt, forgiveness does not allow it to
     ruin the rest of your life. The more you confess
     forgiveness, the less you will feel the sting of the
     pain. Eventually it will become a distant
     memory. When you forgive, the emotions that
     are tied to specific events begin to fade. You can
     be FREE.

If you are a believer, then you know your words have authority
and power! So, speak it out, repent and forgive. It is time for you
to enjoy your best life.

Do you want to know something? You do not have to have a
relationship with everyone you have forgiven. You can genuinely
forgive and move on and they don't have to be a part of your life.
One day when I was writing this book, I was reminded of a quote
that said, "You don't have to have a relationship with everyone
you've forgiven." All I could say was "Amen. Thank you, Lord."

The problem is that a lot of people think that just because you forgive a person they get to come back into your life or inner circle. NOT TRUE! The Lord wants us to walk in love and forgive, but not subject yourself to unnecessary drama or heartache.

Forgiveness means that you have made peace with the pain, and you are ready to let it go; moving forward with your life. Whether it's a spouse who was unfaithful, a parent who let you down, or a friend who shared something private, we must forgive.

MISCONCEPTIONS ABOUT FORGIVENESS

JOURNALING SESSION

Take the time to write down what forgiveness means to you. Who taught you what you believe about forgiveness? Why do you believe that this definition of forgiveness is true?

_____

_____

_____

_____

To learn how to forgive, you must first know what forgiveness is not. Most of us hold at least some misconceptions about forgiveness. Here are some things that forgiving someone doesn't mean:

- You are pardoning or excusing the other person's actions.
- You need to tell the person that he or she is forgiven.
- You shouldn't have any more feelings about the situation.
- There will be nothing further to work out in the relationship or that everything is okay now.
- You should forget the incident ever happened.

- You have to continue to include the person in your life.
- Forgiveness is something that you do for the other person.

By forgiving, you are accepting the reality of what happened and finding a way to live in a state of resolution with the outcome. I know that you're thinking "but how do you go about doing this?" Know that this will be a gradual process. It doesn't necessarily have to include the person you are forgiving. Forgiveness isn't something you do for the person who wronged you; it's something you do for you. So if forgiveness is something you do for yourself and if it can help you heal, why is it so hard?

MOMENT OF REFLECTION

Journaling Session: Before moving on to the next section, take some time to write down in your journal or notebook the reasons why you feel that forgiveness is hard?

_____

_____

_____

_____

_____

There may be several reasons: Search your heart and be honest with yourself to see if you fit any of these categories. If you do, its ok. Remember it's a process.

- You're filled with thoughts of retribution or revenge
- You don't believe God will vindicate you, or that His vindication isn't enough
- You enjoy feeling superior
- You think that if you forgive they won't feel the pain you felt
- You don't know how to resolve the situation
- You're addicted to the adrenaline that anger provides

- You self-identify as a "victim"
- You're afraid that by forgiving you have to re-connect or lose your connection.

Now that you know what forgiveness is not and why it's been so hard, ask yourself: Do I want to forgive?

> *For if you forgive others their trespasses [their reckless and willful sins], your heavenly Father will also forgive you. But if you do not forgive others [nurturing your hurt and anger with the result that it interferes with your relationship with God], then your Father will not forgive your trespasses.*
>
> **Matthew 6:14-16 AMP**

Ask yourself, what could it cost me if I choose not to forgive?

JOURNALING SESSION

Take some time to write down what it will cost you to forgive vs. not forgiving.

_____

_____

_____

_____

By forgiving and forgetting, you are allowing yourself to *prevent* the roots of bitterness, resentment and hate from taking up residence in your heart. When you forgive you allow the Lord our God, to do the healing and restoration. It's a pain that only God can take away. Think about that for a moment. Now ask yourself that question again. Why hold on to past hurts? Take a deep breath. You are going to be alright—just breathe.

Forgiveness requires a willingness to let go. Sometimes we believe we can't because the pain is too deep. Always remember, forgiveness is a choice that has eternal consequences, so don't take it lightly. This moment and these decisions are all for YOU.

THE PATH TO FORGIVENESS

If you are willing to forgive and want to work toward your healing, set aside some time to be alone with your thoughts. Then, try following these four steps to forgive even when it feels impossible.

Don't forget to take out your journal or notebook to use as you work through the steps below.

1. Think about the incident that angered or hurt you. Accept that it happened. Accept how you felt about it and how it made you react. To forgive, you need to acknowledge the reality of what occurred and how you were affected. Your feelings matter! This helps to identify where you are. But we aren't going to stay in our feelings. It's ok to cry. God promised to bottle up every tear and there is no Comforter like the Holy Spirit.

2. Acknowledge the growth you experienced as a result of what happened. What did it make you learn about yourself or about your needs and boundaries? Not only did you survive the incident, perhaps you grew from it. Every disappointment, trial, or situation has a lesson

in it. Pay attention. Start asking God the right
questions.

3. Now think about the other person. He or she is
    flawed because all human beings are flawed.
    He/She/They acted from limited beliefs and a
    skewed frame of reference. Sometimes we all
    operate from our limited views and skewed
    frames of reference. When you were hurt, the
    other person was trying to have a need met.
    What do you think this need was and why did
    the person go about it in such a hurtful way?

4. Finally, decide whether or not you want to tell
    the other person that you have forgiven them. If
    you choose not to express forgiveness directly,
    then do it on your own. Say the words, "I
    forgive you" aloud and then add as much
    explanation as you feel is merited.

Understand that forgiveness puts the final seal on the painful
experience that hurt you. You will still remember what happened,
but it will no longer bind you. Working through those feelings
and learning your boundaries will enable you to take better care
of your emotional well-being. Forgiving the other person is a
beautiful way to honor yourself. It affirms that you deserve to be
happy.

When you forgive, you are preventing the roots of bitterness, resentment, and hate from taking residence in your heart. Allow the Lord, our God to complete the healing and restoration process. He is the ONLY one that can take it away. Forgive and let go of grudges and bitterness. Don't leave these wounds untreated, go through the process of cleansing and healing. Remember this, one drop of poison can kill, so imagine drinking a gallon. That's what we do every time we let unforgiveness go unchecked, we keep drinking the poison.

Let's be free, get free and live free. Since Jesus has already paid the price, why not take advantage of the freedom that was gifted to you? Repent for your part, because you may have held on too long. Take some time today to repent for the role that you played in the situation. If you can't see where you played a part, ask the Holy Spirit to reveal it to you.

SECTION 3 – GRAB HOLD OF FAITH

You have to forgive by faith. You have to be willing to release, trust and believe that God is truly who He says He is: the healer and restorer. He alone will perfect that which concerns you.

We all know of someone who refused to forgive until they received an apology first. You might have even been that "someone." Apologizing does not always mean that you were wrong. Sometimes it is the bridge to diffuse chaos, bring order to disorder and possibly mend the fences. It's not always about who's right and who is wrong, that's pride. When you walk with Jesus, you give up the need to "be right" for the power to be righteous (walking in Holiness and integrity). Right is your way. Righteous (morally justified) is God's way. Let's choose righteousness so we can experience the freedom we were made for.

You may not agree with everything talked about in this book, and that's ok. Walking in forgiveness may be new to you. I want you to take some time to reflect on all the things we've talked about so far.

JOURNALING SESSION

Why do you think it's important to the healing process? How can walking in Faith make a difference? Why is forgiveness a faith walk for you?

_____

_____

_____

_____

SECTION 4 – HOW TO FORGIVE AND TAKE THE NEXT STEP FORWARD

We've all been hurt at some point and time; while this pain is normal, sometimes it lingers a bit too long. We may replay the pain and offense over and over and have a hard time letting go. This has caused many of us problems. It not only robs us of the joy and peace God intended for us; it can ruin relationships. It becomes a distraction from work, family and other important things. This may cause you to be reluctant to open up to new ideas and people. When we get trapped in a cycle of anger and hurt, we could miss out on the beauty of life as it's happening.

We must learn to let go and let God.

This is something I learned the hard way. Growing up, I experienced emotional, physical, and mental abuse. I held on to this anger for years. When I finally decided to let it go (about eight years ago or so), my relationships improved and caused me to be happier.

Forgiveness will change your life, it may not change theirs and you have to be ok with that. Forgiveness does not mean you erase the past or forget what has happened. It doesn't even mean the other person will change his/her behavior . . . you cannot control that. All it means is that you are letting go of the anger and pain, and moving on to a better place. It's not easy, but you can learn to do it. Here's some tips on how you can move forward:

Make a commitment. By now you realize it's going to be a process. It can take time to get over something. So commit to changing, because you recognize that the pain is hurting you. Also, be proud of yourself for wanting to be free and taking the steps to get there.

Think about the pros and cons. What problems does this pain cause you? Does it affect your relationships? Does it affect your work? Your family? Does it stop you from pursuing your dreams or becoming a better person? Does it cause you unhappiness?

Take some time to write in your journal and make a note of anything that comes to mind or your heart pertaining to this.

1.   Next, think of the benefits of forgiveness. How will it make you happier? What would it feel like to be free from the past and the pain. It will propel you towards your purpose because now you are free to hear clearly from God. Unforgiveness blocks your communication with God.

2.   Realize that you have a choice. You cannot control the actions of others and shouldn't try to. You can control your actions and thoughts. You can stop reliving the hurt and choose to move on. You have the power to move forward and free yourself.

3.   Empathize. Try this: put yourself in that person's shoes. Try to understand why the person did what they did. Start from the assumption that the person isn't a bad person, but just did something wrong. What could they have been thinking? What could have happened to them in the past to make them do what they did? What did they feel afterward? How they feel now? You are not condoning what they did

but instead are trying to understand and empathize.

4. Understand your responsibility. Try to figure out how you could have been partially responsible for what happened. What could you have done differently? How can you prevent it from happening next time? This isn't to say you're taking the blame, or taking responsibility away from the other person. In some cases we aren't always the victim, but have been willing participants.

5. Focus on the present. You've had time to reflect on the past, and you're working on letting it go. Now the work is in your mind. No longer allow it to replay and reseed your heart. Instead, bring your focus back to the present moment. What are you doing now? What joy can you find in what is happening right now? Find the joy in life now and stop reliving the past. If your mind takes you back there gently bring yourself back to the present.

6. Allow peace to enter your life. Let's try an exercise. As you focus on the present, try focusing on your breathing. Imagine each time

you breathe out, envision the pain and the past,
being released from your body and mind.
Imagine each breath coming in is peace entering
and filling you up. Exhale and release it. Let
peace enter your life. Go forward; slowly let the
thoughts slip away as you bring your mind back
to a peaceful state and reset. All you have to do
is believe that it's possible, then God will take
care of the rest.

As you are doing this exercise, you could even listen to some good
meditation, relaxation, or instrumental worship music to help relax
your mind. Here are a few links to some music that I recommend.

Here In Your Presence – Deep Prayer Music:
**https://www.youtube.com/watch?v=zs6
_X6enClk&list=RDzs6_X6enClk**

Holy Spirit – 1 Hour Deep Prayer:
https://www.youtube.com/watch?v=WME1N9A64Qg

Peace – 2 Hours of Piano Worship:
https://www.youtube.com/watch?v=mNMdGy41PJQ

Comfort & Healing – 3 Hour Peaceful Music:
**https://www.youtube.com/watch?v=pN36slk_R24&list
=RDpN36slk_R24**

Healing Bible Scriptures and Soaking Music:
https://www.youtube.com/watch?v=1wfewVsIdf0

Feel compassion. Finally, forgive the person and realize that in forgiveness, you are allowing yourself to be happy and move on. Feel empathy for the person and wish blessings on them. Let love for them and for life in general to grow in your heart. It may take time, if you find this step difficult, repeat some of the steps above until you can get here.

RELEASE THE HURT

When you hurt, don't hold it in. When we hold onto hurt because we think we can handle it, we are allowing seeds to take root. All it takes is another hurt to cause bitterness to grow and manifest. Before you know it, you have a harvest rooted in bitterness, jealousy and anger. Some of us are quick to say, "I forgive quickly!" It is not until that next hurt comes, in the same area, that we realize that we haven't truly forgiven or healed properly. That's a familiar spirit. Dig that thang up! Yes, I said thang because we must get down and dirty to dig up the root once and for all. These are not my words. God is the one that says NOTHING is impossible with Him.

> *Jesus looked at them intently and said, "Humanly speaking, it is impossible. But not with God. Everything is possible with God."*
> **Mark 10:27 NLT**

Now, Jesus did say confess your faults one to another and pray for one another and lift them up in prayer so you can be healed.

Cast Your Cares: Time to get vulnerable

God wants you to throw your cares on Him. Relinquish every weight, thought, concern, and struggle and throw them towards Him. That means you must be willing to be vulnerable. This journey is between you and God. He's the one who can change all things. You can talk to Him, cry in front of Him, scream, laugh whatever you need. He will lovingly comfort, refresh and restore you.

> *Give all your worries and cares to God, for he cares about you.*
>
> **1 Peter 5:7 NLT**

He will bless you publicly for what you release to Him in private. Ask God to help you quiet your mind and remember any unforgiveness you have in your heart. Repent for any areas that He shows you, then let it go.

> *Dear brothers and sisters, if another believer is overcome by some sin, you who are godly should gently and humbly help that person back onto the right path. And be careful not to fall into the same temptation yourself. Share each other's burdens, and in this way obey the law of Christ. If you think you are too important to help someone, you are only fooling yourself. You are not that important.*
>
> **Galatians 6:1-3 NLT**

There is power in forgiveness. There is power in agreement. Sometimes you just need someone to come alongside you. Someone that has spiritual maturity and loves God more than man! You need someone that isn't going to get all in your business. Someone who is going to listen and only speak the Word. Someone who will keep their opinions out of it, pray, then praise God with you that it's done.

Know that I am so proud of you!! This is hard work and you are doing that thang.

You've got this, I've got you, but more importantly God's got you!

SECTION 5 – WALKING IN FORGIVENESS

Walking in forgiveness is such a powerful way to change your life. The power of forgiveness is in its simplicity! This walk may be used for any issue you may be facing. However, it is best to start with relatively small matters until you get the idea. It may be best not to try and forgive someone who could potentially cause you further hurt until you have some experience and understanding of your forgiveness process.

Let's recap some things we've learned so far . . .

Step 1: State who you need to forgive and for what.

Step 2: Acknowledge how you currently feel about the situation.

Step 3: State the benefits you will get from forgiving.

Step 4: Commit yourself to be forgiving.

Step 5: Commit no longer rehearse the pain and offense.

Let it go.

JOURNALING SESSION

Using your journal, create a sentence about each person you need to forgive and why.

I want to forgive _____ for

_____ .

At the point of writing your sentence, I want you to take a moment to really acknowledge what you are feeling: anger, pain, fear, envy, wanting revenge . . . be honest.

Next, write:

I make the choice to release my feeling(s) of _____ .

I acknowledge that forgiving this situation will benefit me as I will feel _____ .

Take some time to reflect on what you wrote and released. How did it make you feel?

_____

_____

We forgive because we are forgiven. Jesus paid the ultimate sacrifice by willingly laying His life down. Because of this act of love we are saved and forgiven for our sins (past, present and future. How awesome is that! All we have to do is believe, confess and repent. Ask for forgiveness, believe you are forgiven, and it is done.

If the Lord freely and deliberately forgives us when we confess our sins, who are we not to forgive. Obedience is always better than sacrifice. Obedience is doing what God wants; sacrifice is doing what you want.

> *A final word: Be strong in the Lord and in his mighty power. Put on all of God's armor so that you will be able to stand firm against all strategies of the devil. For we are not fighting against flesh-and-blood enemies, but against evil rulers and authorities of the unseen world, against mighty powers in this dark world, and against evil spirits in the heavenly places. Therefore, put on every piece of God's armor so you will be able to resist the enemy in the time of evil. Then after the battle you will still be standing firm. Stand your ground, putting on the belt of truth and the body armor of God's righteousness. For shoes, put on the peace that comes from the Good News so that you will be fully prepared, In addition to all of these, hold up the shield of faith to stop the fiery arrows of the devil.*

*Put on salvation as your helmet, and take the sword
of the Spirit, which is the word of God. Pray in the
Spirit at all times and on every occasion. Stay alert
and be persistent in your prayers for all believers
everywhere And pray for me, too. Ask God to give
me the right words so I can boldly explain God's
mysterious plan that the Good News is for Jews and
Gentiles alike.*

Ephesians 6:10-19 NLT

You must recognize who the offender is behind the scenes of your hurt. Remember we wrestle not against flesh and blood. You must identify the demonic forces that are determined to destroy your peace and purpose by locking you into unforgiveness.

I can tell you first hand that if it wasn't for the power of forgiveness in my life; receiving it from God and in releasing forgiveness to others, I would literally be dead or in jail . . . I'm just saying. I realize sometimes people will try you. We just need to forgive and leave folks alone. You never know when someone is at their breaking point. Forgiving and being forgiven restores your joy, sense of inner peace, integrity, and overall well-being.

Forgiveness has a beautiful, yet an elusive quality. It involves being honest enough to face what has happened and allow justice to stand tall in love. As I mentioned in previous chapters, forgiveness does not mean letting people walk all over us. We will take action for our lives and step forward with a new approach one step at a time. We will no longer carry our shame like a scarlet letter on our hearts. God's arms are forever open in forgiveness. Our humility comes when we realize that we too have made mistakes, therefore, we must also forgive others as Christ has forgiven us. Remember that there is nothing anyone can do to you that wasn't first already known by God. God is just waiting on you to acknowledge it and release it, so that you can go to your NEXT LEVEL.

EXERCISE

Take out a sheet of paper and write out three major things that have offended you or that you haven't let go. Now write the date of the offense next to it. How long have you been carrying the offense? The offense that you made note of is unforgiveness. You are the only one in mental jail. Reread the offenses that you wrote and say the date out loud so that you can truly hear how long you have kept yourself in bondage. How long have you been walking in spiritual, mental and emotional circles because you wouldn't forgive or receive forgiveness? Remember, it's always your choice. We all have free will.

But today, it's over . . . now tear up the paper and pray these words:

PRAYER

"Lord, I'm presenting myself to You with my hands lifted high. I present to you my heart because You know what's been hurting me. I repent for carrying the weight of unforgiveness and boarding up my heart, with the nails of offense. I held on too long. Comfort me Holy Spirit as I lay it all out before You. Free me. By faith, I receive my forgiveness so that I can be free to forgive others, in Jesus Name."

Now, let's keep walking . . . Be Blessed!

ABOUT THE AUTHOR

TIKESHA MCNULTY affectionately known as Kesha, is a wife, mother of two beautiful daughters and two sons, GlamMa to one beautiful granddaughter. She played Women's' Professional Football, and a US Army Veteran. Kesha is also the founder of a non-profit organization, Hope in Hearts, with more than 25 years of advocacy and community involvement in serving underserved communities and at-risk populations. Through her volunteer efforts and non-profit ventures, she has dedicated her life to empowering people through service and prayer.

In addition to Hope in Hearts, Kesha is the Founder and CEO of the apparel company, 4 The Body, which focuses on uplifting lives through impactful and empowering designs and slogans.

Over the last few years, she has found her real passion as a Forgiveness coach, empowering people to forgive others. Kesha has authored two books: "Forgiven" and "Hadassah's Anointing." She is also a co-author of "What is a Courageous Woman?" She oversees several Forgiveness Programs, including a 12-week forgiveness class for survivors of Sex Trafficking and Domestic Violence, a course for First Responders, Police Officers, and Soldiers, and a third course that is a Corporate Training Program focused on forgiveness in business and workplace environments.

Whether designing Christ-centered apparel, mentoring at-risk women & girls, praying for the hopeless, or serving homeless families, She carries her desire to transform the community into the Kingdom like a badge of honor because it is the Father's Heart.

Kesha also serves as Minister of Missions and Outreach in ministry under the Leadership of Pastor Stanley Jay and Pastor Joyce Jay at Worship Life Center Church in Mesa, Arizona.

Kesha and her husband, Christopher McNulty, reside in Arizona.

BIBLE TRANSLATIONS/
ABBREVIATIONS REFERENCES

ABBREVATION	TRANSLATION
(TLV)	Tree of Life Version
(MEV)	Modern English Version
(AMP)	Amplified Bible
(NLT)	New Living Translation

www.ingramcontent.com/pod-product-compliance
Lightning Source LLC
Chambersburg PA
CBHW070810120626
46557CB00002B/790

* 9 7 9 8 9 8 6 9 9 0 7 6 7 *